"DON'T HANG AROUND WITH THE WRONG CROWD!"

CREDITS

Producer
  Ron Berry

Editor
  Orly Kelly

What to do
when your mom or dad says ...
"DON'T HANG AROUND
WITH THE WRONG CROWD!"
By
JOY BERRY

GROLIER ENTERPRISES CORP.

Has your mother or father ever told you . . .

When your parents tell you that you cannot be around someone, do you feel frustrated and angry? Do you ever wonder...

If any of this sounds familiar to you, you are going to **love** this book!

Because it will tell you exactly why your parents are concerned about whom you spend time with. It will also tell you what you can do to develop and maintain positive relationships.

The word *peer* means "equal" or "the same."

Peer groups are groups in which the people share the same age, general thoughts, interests and behavior.

Being around people who are not like you could cause problems. For example, you might find it frustrating to belong to an adult peer group. This is because you would not think or act like anyone in the group. This might cause you to wonder...

If you belonged to an adult peer group, you would probably not want to do the things that the group wanted to do. This is because you would not think or act like the people in the group.

Thus, it is normal for you to want to be around people who are similar to you.

It is good for you to spend time with people who think and act somewhat as you do.

BELONGING TO A PEER GROUP CAN BE GOOD FOR YOU

Belonging to a peer group can help you to overcome loneliness.

It can provide you with activities and experiences that can be done only in a group.

When you belong to a peer group, you will not feel left out or rejected.

Peer groups can help you to feel accepted.

By being with people who are a lot like you, you learn more about who you are and how other people see you.

MY MOM CONSTANTLY NAGS AT ME TO CLEAN MY ROOM. I CAN'T UNDERSTAND WHY I CAN'T KEEP IT THE WAY I WANT TO KEEP IT!

ITS THE SAME BETWEEN MY PARENTS AND ME. WE FIGHT ABOUT IT ALL THE TIME!

YEAH!

REALLY

You also learn that you are not different from others or strange. You discover that most of your thoughts, feelings and actions are normal and healthy.

Sometimes it is easier for you to share thoughts and questions with your peers. This is because they think and wonder about the same things you do. Thus, you know that they will not put you down for the way you think and feel.

When you feel that you are being mistreated, you may want to be around people who feel the same way. This is because you think that their experiences will help them to understand you. You may find comfort and support in talking with them.

BELONGING TO A PEER GROUP CAN HARM YOU

You might not be **exactly** like the people in your peer group. This may bother the individuals in the group. Your being different might cause them to wonder if something is wrong with them. To prove to themselves that they are OK, they may try to get you to be exactly like them.

This could be very harmful. If your peer group wants you to be someone you are not, something is wrong. You must never allow a group to decide how you will think and act. You must make these decisions for yourself.

When the members of your peer group decide to do something, they will most likely want you to do it too. If they decide to do something wrong, they will probably want you to be a part of it. So that you won't feel guilty, they might tell you, "Everyone is doing it, so it can't be bad." You might agree.

This could be very harmful. You are to blame anytime you do something that is wrong. It does not matter whether you are alone or with someone. You must never do something wrong just because your peer group wants you to.

People working together are stronger than a person working alone. When the members of your peer group are doing something together, they may feel strong and powerful. These feelings might cause them to do things that they wouldn't do by themselves.

This could be harmful. Your peer group might decide to use its strength and power to hurt people or to damage or destroy property. If this happens, you must not participate. You should never do anything that would hurt another person or damage or destroy property.

Because you share similar problems, you and your peers may complain a lot when you are together. A certain amount of complaining is good, as it gets problems out in the open where they can be worked on.

However, too much complaining can be harmful. It can make problems seem bigger than they really are. Thinking that your problems are getting worse instead of better could cause you to become sad and depressed. Thus, your peer group is not helping you if it allows you to complain without helping you to solve your problems.

It is natural to become like the people you spend a lot of time with. Sometimes this can happen without your knowing about it. You may begin to think and act like your peers regardless of how you may feel. In this way, your peer group may be in control of you.

This could be very harmful. You should never allow a group of people to control you. You should never let anyone do your thinking for you. It is up to you to make your own decisions and to live your own life.

CHOOSING THE RIGHT PEER GROUP

Thus, a peer group can help you or harm you. Make sure you are part of a group that helps you.

Here are some questions to consider before joining a peer group:

- Do these people like me for myself?

- Do these people think that my thoughts and
feelings are important?

– Do these people say and do things to make me feel good about myself?

– Is my relationship with these people causing me to become a better person?

- Do the things I do with these people help others around us?

– **Do these people cause me to think good things about others?**

– **Do these people and I have common interests and goals?**

– Is it easy to think of positive things to do
when I am with these people?

– Are these people fun to be with?

- **Am I relaxed when I am around these people?**

CHANGING PEER GROUPS

If you cannot answer yes to most of these questions, you are with the wrong peer group.

If you decide that you must leave a peer group, do it slowly.

Begin by finding a new group to be a part of. You may need to begin with one or two people.

Begin spending time with the new group a little at a time.

Become more and more unavailable to the group you want to leave.

Try not to hold a grudge against the group you left. Forgive them for the things they did to hurt you and then forget it. Don't say bad things about them to other people.

Enjoy and appreciate the peer group that contributes to your life in a positive way. Do your share in making the group a positive one to be in.

THE END of hanging around with the wrong crowd!